the *true art* of stringing PEARLS

COLLECTING THE MOMENTS THAT MATTER

MAGGIE JAMIESON

The True Art of Stringing Pearls:
Collecting the Moments that Matter
BY MAGGIE JAMIESON

Copyright © 2017 Maggie Jamieson. All rights reserved. Except for brief quotations for review purposes, no part of this book may be reproduced in any form without prior written permission from the author.

Published by:

PO BOX 1072
Pinehurst, TX 77362
LifeWiseBooks.com

Interior Layout and Design | Yvonne Parks | PearCreative.ca

To contact the author:
www.MaggieJamieson.org

ISBN (Print): 978-1-947279-16-2
ISBN (Ebook): 978-1-947279-17-9

Dedication

To my husband, Jim
My partner in crime, My best friend.

To my children, Drew and Emma
Two beautiful gifts, My loves.

To my Aunt, Marie Sperduti
Whose constant example of love and acceptance has been forever imprinted on my heart.

TABLE OF CONTENTS

Introduction	7
1 – Pearls of Blessing	11
2 – Pearls of Brokenness	13
3 – Pearls of Change	15
4 – Pearls of Child-like Faith	17
5 – Pearls of a Confident Heart	19
6 – Pearls of Courage	23
7 – Pearls of Covenant	27
8 – Pearls of Discernment	31
9 – Pearls of Encouragement	33
10 – Pearls of Faith	35
11 – Pearls of the Father's Heart	37
12 – Pearls of Freedom of Choice	41
13 – Pearls of Forgiveness	45
14 – Pearls of Grace	49
15 – Pearls of Heaven's Breath	51
16 – Pearls of Honor	53
17 – Pearls of Identity	57
18 – Pearls of Jesus' Love	61
19 – Pearls of Kindness	63
20 – Pearls of Mercy	67
21 – Pearls of a New Name	69
22 – Pearls of Obedience	71
23 – Pearls of Our Words	73
24 – Pearls of Overcoming Distress	77

25 – Pearls of Peace	81
26 – Pearls of Perspective	83
27 – Pearls of Presence	85
28 – Pearls of Provision	87
29 – Pearls of Purpose	91
30 – Pearls of Resurrection Power	93
31 – Pearls of Righteousness	95
32 – Pearls of Seeking Justice	99
33 – Pearls of Self-Care	103
34 – Pearls of Service	105
35 – Pearls of Surrender	107
36 – Pearls of Transformation	111
37 – Pearls of Trust	115
38 – Pearls of Togetherness	117
39 – Pearls of Unity	119
40 – Pearls of Victory	121
41 – Pearls of Vow-Making	125
42 – Pearls of Worth	127
About the Author	129

INTRODUCTION

The Strand

Stringing pearls is an art that comes from embracing the rhythm of one's journey. Life provides a never-ending series of events that when analyzed, are like pearls. No two are alike yet they are all valuable and beautiful when strung together. The strand is where we collect and remember these treasures. Recognizing the pearls and organizing them in our hearts is an art.

The strand is strengthened by our connection with God. It holds these precious gifts together in the balance, which is why it is imperative to integrate God in the stringing process.

Allow Him to guide your interpretation of events in your life. Pray that He will speak life over dormant areas in your heart. Pray that He will bring restoration to damaged or broken places.

The result of passing each event through God's filter will be a beautiful strand of pearls that are uniquely yours.

> *"Though one may be overpowered, two can defend themselves. A cord of three strands is not quickly broken."*[1]

The Pearls

To think that one irritating, tiny grain of sand can cultivate a radiant and miraculous pearl within the oyster is amazing. The sand actually injures the oyster, despite the opulent outcome of the injury.

A pearl is a beautiful gift produced by an injured life. It is the tear that results from the injury of the oyster. The treasure of our being in this world is often a product of an injury we sustain. If we have not been wounded, if we have not been injured, then we cannot produce or cultivate the pearl.

Finding the Pearls

Identifying these precious treasures is an art in and of itself. It is a skill worth developing so that we don't discount the value of our experiences both good and bad.

To see these treasures, we must first have vision. This is simply the ability to see what is just below the surface of our circumstances. Second, faith to believe that God has a purpose for every detail of our lives. Third is courage to become all that God designed us to be. And finally, we must stand firm and remain rooted in the promises of God over our lives.

There isn't always a neat and tidy order in which these experiences come either. To honor that, I have included a variety of pearls I have come across in my life. My hope is that this collection will help you see the beauty in your own life's experiences and cherish the collective value of it.

ENDNOTE

1. Ephesians 4:12

1
pearls of blessing

In February of 2016, my daughter, Emma, found out she would be receiving a wish from the *Make a Wish CT*.

That one wish literally was a game changer. Not just for myself, but for Emma, who is the strongest person I have ever known. From my son, Drew, to my husband Jim and I, we all have definitely been affected by her profound illness.

I was so moved by this blessing from the foundation: a family trip to London and Paris. In April of 2016, we arrived in

London, tired but excited. Emma and I had our own room, and after dinner, we watched the show, *Britain's Got Talent*.

A young girl performed a powerful rendition of the song "Defying Gravity" from the Broadway show, *Wicked*. I was moved to tears by the sheer bravery it must have taken this young girl to perform in front of such a large crowd.

When the performance was over, Emma turned to me and said; "Mom, maybe you and I can defy gravity, together'" More tears. We were so blessed.

> "The Lord bless you and keep you; the Lord make his face shine on you and be gracious to you; the Lord turn his face toward you and give you peace."[1]

ENDNOTE

1. Numbers 6:24-26

2
pearls of brokenness

If you drop a glass mug and it shatters, then glue every single piece back together, it will never go back to its original state. It is forever changed. This is the limitation of things in the tangible world.

However, as a child of God, when our lives are broken in pieces, God's restoration makes us better than we were before the damage was done. We may still carry the memories of the injury, but we don't have to remain broken.

The breaking becomes part of our story, our testimony, and through our testimony we rise in beauty from the ashes. We can share with others, not only from a place of having been broken, but also from the place of restoration.

As we see in Joel 2:25, God can restore what is broken and changed it into something amazing. All you need is faith.

3
pearls of change

The past doesn't equal the future. It's in the moment of decision that your destiny is shaped. Whatever you think about most you'll experience. The fastest way to change how you feel about anything is to change what you're focusing on.

> *"If you want to succeed in your life, remember this phrase: That past does not equal the future. Because you failed yesterday; or all day today; or a moment ago; or for the last six months; the last sixteen years; or the last fifty years of life, doesn't*

mean anything… All that matters is: What are you going to do, right now?"[1]

You can change anything in your life today by changing your perceptions and your actions.

The key to successful change is to decide what's most important to you and then take massive action each day to make it better, even when it doesn't look as if it's working. Ultimately, it's our decisions, rather than the conditions of our lives, that determine our destiny.

Often, the reason people say they can't do something is that they've tried things in the past that have not worked. What matters is not yesterday, but what you do right now. Every time you do something, you learn from it, and you find a way to do it better next time.

ENDNOTES

1. Robbins, Anthony. Positively Positive.com. http://www.positivelypositive.com/?s=Anthony+Robbins&post_type=quotes. Accessed 24 June 2017.

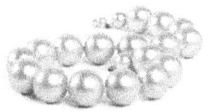

4
pearls of child-like faith

When I was about six years old; my parents took us to see Santa, at Christmas time. We waited in the long line; one by one, my siblings and I got to sit on Santa's lap. When it was my turn, Santa asked me what I wanted for Christmas. "Nothing;" I replied. Santa encouraged me; "Surely there is something you want?"

I thought for a moment and blurted out, "An orange." My mother was horrified. Santa said; "If you're a good girl, I'm sure you'll receive it." I had childlike faith. That Christmas morning;

to my surprise, guess what one of my gifts from Santa was? An orange! I will never forget the moment I opened that gift. It is forever sketched across my heart.

> *"And He said: Truly I tell you, unless you change and become like little children, you will never enter the kingdom of heaven."*[1]

> *"This is the confidence we have in approaching God: that if we ask anything according to His will, He hears us."*[2]

ENDNOTES

1. Matthew 18:3
2. 1 John 5:14

5
pearls of confident heart

A confident heart is a byproduct of a mended heart. Not one single thing in your life is wasted. God will use your past and present to prepare you for your future.

God wants you to have the confidence to ask hard questions and look for answers that usher in His redeeming love.

Confidence is about respecting your own value, worth, and

dignity. Your identity is defined by who God says you are, not what the world says. It's what God says about you that counts.

Remind yourself what the blood of Jesus Christ did for you, and put on the full armor of God daily. Ask the Holy Spirit to baptize you afresh every day. You have the victory, because the enemy has already been defeated. When the enemy comes trying to torment you, remind him he is a defeated foe. Command him to be silent, and cast him out.

> *"When a train goes through a tunnel and it gets dark, you don't throw away your ticket and jump off. You sit still and trust the engineer."* [1]

> *"Finally, be strong in the Lord and in his mighty power. Put on the full armor of God, so that you can take your stand against the devil's schemes. For our struggle is not against flesh and blood, but against the rulers, against the authorities, against the powers of this dark world and against the spiritually forces of evil in the heavenly realms."* [2]

> *"I will give you the treasures of darkness, and hidden wealth of secret places, so that you may know that it is I, the Lord, who calls you by name."* [3]

ENDNOTES

1. Ten Boom, Corrie. Brainy Quotes.com, https://www.brainyquote.com/quotes/quotes/c/corrietenb393675.html. Accessed 11 September 2017.

2. Ephesians 6:10-12

3. Isaiah 45:3 (NASB)

6
pearls of courage

"What's the greatest risk? Letting go of what people think or letting go of how I feel, what I believe, and who I am?"[1]

> *"Be strong and courageous. Do not be afraid or terrified because of them, for the Lord your God goes with you: he will never leave you or forsake you."*[2]

- Dare to have courage in your dreams.
- Know your limitations and then defy them.

- Dare to be courageous today.
- Dare to be different.
- We were made to be courageous.
- Courage draws out the greatness that is stored inside us like pearls.
- Dare to be who you truly are.
- Dare to be vulnerable with yourself by embracing all that you are, and trusting God's process.

> "Owning our story and loving ourselves through that process is the bravest thing we'll ever do."[3]

> "The Lord is my light and my salvation- whom shall I fear? The Lord is the stronghold of my life—whom shall I fear?"[4]

> "May God arise, may his enemies be scattered."[5]

ENDNOTES

1. Brown, Brene. "14 Inspirational Quotes from Brene Brown." Happily Imperfect.com, edited by Sharon Martin, Accessed 11 September 2017.

2. Deuteronomy 31:6

3. Brown, Brene. Good Reads.com, https://www.goodreads.com/quotes/330217-i-now-see-how-owning-our-story-and-loving-ourselves. Accessed 11 September 2017.

4. Psalm 27:1

5. Psalm 68:1

7
pearls of covenant

What is a covenant? According to *Webster's Dictionary*, as a noun it is an "agreement," and as a verb, it is "to agree, especially by lease, deed or other legal documents."[1]

As an American, I am reminded of our Declaration of Independence. The Declaration of Independence was America's covenant with God. At the signing of this document on July 4, 1776, we became "One Nation Under God." Fifty-six great Americans signed this document, and many of them paid with their lives and fortunes. That is covenant living at its finest.

In the Bible, a covenant is an agreement between two people or God and his people. God makes promises to his people and usually requires certain conduct from them. In the Old Testament, God made covenants with Noah, Abraham, and Moses.

A covenant is so important to believers because it is an agreement ratified in blood by a God who cannot lie and never abandons what He promises. It is the agreement between two parties, us and God, which is laid out for us in the scriptures. [2]

> *"The angel of the Lord went up from Gilgal to Bokim and said, "I brought you up out of Egypt and led you into the land I swore to give to your ancestors. I said, "I will never break my covenant with you."*[3]
>
> *"For this God is our God, forever and ever. He will be our guide even to the end."*[4]
>
> *"Call to Me, and I will answer you, and show you great and mighty things, which you do not know."*[5]

ENDNOTES

1. "Covenant." Dictionary.com. http://www.dictionary.com/browse/covenant. Accessed 7 September 2017.

2. Genesis 9:13, Genesis 6:18, Deuteronomy 33:9

3. Judges 2:1

4. Psalm 48:14

5. Jeremiah 33:3 (NKJV)

8
pearls of discernment

Discernment is not the difference between right and wrong; it is being able to tell the difference between right and almost right, between what is in alignment and out, between a good relationship and a bad one.

Discerning the season of life you are in helps you understand what God is working to do in your life. Whether it's a season of rain or a season of sunshine, God is using it to shape you and prepare you for the future.

"The moment you began praying, a command was given. And now I am here to tell you what it was, for you are very precious to God. Listen carefully so that you can understand the meaning of your vision." [1]

ENDNOTES

1. Daniel 9:23 (NLT)

9
pearls of encouragement

When you feel inadequate, God says, *"You are chosen"*[1]

When you feel afraid, God says, *"You are redeemed."*[2]

When you feel unloved, God says, *"You are loved."*[3]

When you feel unloved, God says, *"You are remembered."*[4]

When you feel insecure, God says, *"You are secure."*[5]

When you feel unable, God say, *"You are able."*[6]

When you feel worthless, God says, *"You are called."*[7]

> *"'For I know the plans I have for you,' says the Lord. 'They are plans for good and not for disaster, to give you a future and a hope.'"*[8]

ENDNOTES

1. Isaiah 43:10
2. Isaiah 43:1
3. Isaiah 43:4
4. Isaiah 49:16
5. Deuteronomy 33:12
6. Habakkuk 3:19
7. 1 Peter 2:9
8. Jeremiah 29:11

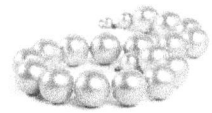

10
pearls of faith

At 75 years old, Abraham receives a call from God. At 75, most people are enjoying their retirement. Abraham had a good life. He had family, a community, and wealth. Yet God was calling him forth into something greater. Against all odds, Abraham believed. It's worth noting that Abraham did not have the Bible to scroll through for confirmation, nor did he have a creed or a religion. He simply heard the call and obeyed.

Sure, his journey was filled with adventures and great mishaps, but by keeping his connection open to God, Abraham became the father of many nations.

> *"In Hope, he believed against hope, that he should become the father of many nations, as he had been told, 'So shall your offspring be.'"* [1]

> *"And He took him outside and said, 'Now look toward the heavens, and count the stars, if are able to count them,' and He said to him, 'So shall your descendants be.'"* [2]

ENDNOTES

1. Romans 4:18 (ESV)
2. Genesis 15:5 (ESV)

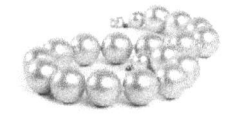

11
pearls of the father's heart

God gave the best He had by giving us his only son. He does not hold back anything that is for our benefit or good.

The story of the prodigal son is a parable demonstrating God the Father's Heart.[1] Here are a few facets of His heart:

"The Father's Heart never loses hope.

The Father's Heart is always looking towards us.

The Father's Heart responds to our repentance.

The Father's Heart wants to reinstate us."[2]

As we grow spiritually, intimacy with our Father's heart grows as well. We will grasp even more how God loves the entire world, every tribe and nation.

> *"He who did not spare His Own Son, but delivered Him up for us all, how shall He not with Him also freely give us all things?"*[3]

> *"For Jehovah God is our Light and our Protector. He gives us grace and glory. No good thing will He withhold from those who walk along his paths."*[4]

> *"And my God shall supply all your needs per His riches in glory by Christ Jesus."*[5]

> *"When you pass through the waters, I will be with you."*[6]

ENDNOTES

1. Luke 15

2. Russell, Pastor Paul. Sermon: Men and God. www.facebook.com/ChristFamilyTV. Accessed June 18, 2017.

3. Romans 8:32 (NKJV)

4. Psalm 84:11 (TLB)

5. Philippians 4:19

6. Isaiah 43:2

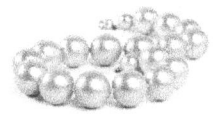

12
pearls of freedom of choice

"What you are is God's gift to you, what you become is your gift to God." [1]

One of the greatest gifts God gave man is the gift of choice, or free will. You have the right to choose to do right or to do wrong. But whatever you choose to do, you must deal with the outcome.

Free will is a wonderful gift from our heavenly father. He is always reaching for us with His righteous right hand. It is our choice to reach back out to Him.

I tell you from experience, it's easier to just do right. Your journey is a testimony to the freedom of choice, and we are all equally granted the ability to be good on earth and offer help to those in need.

> "You, my brothers and sisters, were called to be free. But do not use your freedom to indulge the flesh; rather, serve one another humbly in love."[2]

> "This day I call the heavens and the earth as witnesses against you that I have set before you, life and death, blessings and curses. Now choose life so that you and your children may live and that you may love the Lord your God, listen to his voice, and hold fast to him. For the Lord is your life, and he will give you many years in the land he swore to your fathers, Abraham, Isaac and Jacob."[3]

> "Create in me a clean heart, O God, and renew a steadfast spirit within me."[4]

ENDNOTES

1. Von Balthasar, Hans Urs. Good Reads.com, https://www.goodreads.com/author/quotes/30796.Hans_Urs_von_Balthasar. Accessed 11 September 2017.

2. Galatians 5:13

3. Deuteronomy 31:19-29

4. Psalm 51:10

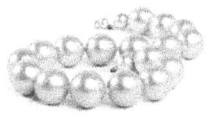

13
pearls of forgiveness

Seventy times seven is a whole lot of forgiveness. I believe the point Jesus was making when he shared this mathematic equation was that there should be no limit to how many times we offer our forgiveness. After all, He is faithful to forgive us EVERY time we ask. So, who are we to place a limit?

I was at a birthday party for my niece, Sophie, back in April of 2015. Technically, I am not her aunt, but I have been friends with her mother, Stacey, since I was a teenager.

At the party, Stacey's grandmother came over to me. She said, "Margaret, I need to speak with you." While I listened intently to her, she told me she needed my forgiveness. I had not seen her in a few years, so I just listened. I was nervous, yet intrigued to hear what she had to say.

Her husband, Stacey's grandfather, had passed away back when I was in high school, and I attended the funeral with Stacey. Apparently, she had scolded me for attending the funeral. That happened so long ago that I honestly had forgotten.

I was fine and told her it was okay, but she continued to talk about it. It was then I realized that allowing her to say what she needed to say wasn't for my benefit, but for hers. She needed to release herself. She told me every time she heard the name Margaret she would get upset because it reminded her of how she hurt me.

I couldn't believe she had been carrying around that weight for so long. When she was finished, I thanked her for that heartfelt apology and hugged her. She looked like that weight had lifted from her shoulders. All I did was listen and forgive, God did the rest. Complete forgiveness brings double honor and allows us to become whole.

"For if you forgive other people when they sin against you, your heavenly Father will also forgive you. But if you do not forgive others their sins, your Father will not forgive your sins." [1]

ENDNOTES

1. Matthew 6:14-15

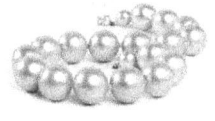

14
pearls of grace

What's most amazing about God is His grace. He gives us grace we don't deserve while not withholding His mercy.

When I was 16 years old, I was very suicidal due to suffering years of severe trauma. Things seemed so dark, and searching for hope seemed fruitless. One Tuesday night, I attended a Bible study at my church. I had given my heart to the Lord a year prior, but that night, I was planning to commit suicide. No one knew but God and myself. I remember calling out to God for help.

When I was leaving church, I accidentally dropped my Bible. A small, white piece of paper fell out that I had never seen before. All that was written on it was: Deuteronomy 31:19. I did not know who had placed that paper within my Bible.

I looked it up and this is what it said:

> *"This day I call the heavens and the earth as witnesses against you that I have set before you life and death, blessings and curses. Now choose life so that you and your children may live and that you may love the Lord your God, listen to his voice, and hold fast to him. For the Lord is your life, and he will give you many years in the land he swore to your fathers, Abraham, Isaac and Jacob."* [1]

That day, I chose LIFE and in doing so, my children received life.

Trust in the goodness of our Father and have faith. Jesus already knows us better than we know ourselves. Keep your mind pure before Him, and receive His grace that is so undeserved.

> *"Grace and Peace be yours in abundance through the knowledge of God and of Jesus our Lord."* [2]

ENDNOTES

1. Deuteronomy 31:19-20

2. 2 Peter 1:2

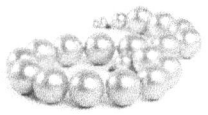

15
pearls of heaven's breath

> *"Then the Lord God formed a man from the dust of the ground and breathed into his nostrils the breath of life, and the man became a living being."[1]*

Man was created by God from the dust, but did not become a living being until God breathed into him the breath of life.

> *"Awake, north wind, and come south wind! Blow on my garden, that its fragrance may spread*

> *everywhere. Let my beloved come into this garden and taste its choice fruits."* [2]

The wind, or breath of God's spirit, blows over us so we can bear His fruit, to bring Him glory.

We need the breath of God to carry the weight of His presence in our everyday lives and spread His love around.

The pearl is learning to walk with the wind of His Presence by walking in His holiness.

> *"I will stand my watch and station myself at the ramparts; I will look to see what he will say to me, and what answer I am to give to this complaint."*[3]

ENDNOTES

1. Genesis 2:7
2. Song of Songs 4:16
3. Habakkuk 2:1

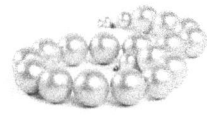

16
pearls of honor

On August 8, 2016, Denny Cramer, who operates in the prophetic gifting, was holding a conference at my home church. He delivered a powerful sermon from Isaiah 61. I asked the Lord what He wanted me to receive, and this is what I heard:

> *Instead of your shame, you will receive a double portion. And instead of disgrace, you will rejoice in your inheritance. And so you*

> *will inherit a double portion in your land,*
> *And everlasting joy will be yours.* [1]

I wrote this in my Bible alongside Isaiah 61:7-11: "double honor: whole/ full/ complete. Complete forgiveness."

This may just be a coincidence, but I felt the need to get my grandfather's medals he had earned in the military. He retired as lieutenant colonel from the army. I also have a letter from President Ronald Reagan thanking my grandfather for his life's service to our country. The letter is framed and hanging in my living room.

This reminded me of "double honor." My grandfather served our country during three conflicts: WW2, Korea, and Vietnam. My grandfather was a "lifer" because he spent his entire working life in the military. He passed away on the 4th of July, 1986, mowing his grass and enjoying his retirement. He was laid to rest at Massachusetts National Cemetery with full military honors. Attending his funeral was a profound experience to have as a teenager.

Now, my son Drew has enlisted in the military. As a mother, I experience fear because of how the world looks today. But I am also very proud. I tried to talk Drew out of the military years ago, but who am I to quash his passion? I've embraced it. Last Christmas, I asked him for the last time why he wants to join the marines. His answer to me awe-inspiring. Drew said,

"Mom, Israel needs to be defended, at all costs." I was humbled and amazed at his passion.

ENDNOTES

1. Isaiah 61:7

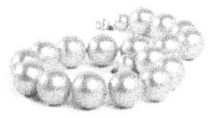

17
pearls of identity

The pearls of identity are:

Our passion – So that we may display courage and enjoy life.

Our integrity – So that we may display honor.

Our quality – So that we may display discipline.

Our transparency – So that we may feel the power of being vulnerable.

Identity cannot be found or fabricated but emerges from within when you have the courage to let go. Don't let your struggle become your identity. You are "greater than" because of Christ.

When writing the story of your life, let God hold the pen. You are the one who choses what role you play in life. Victim or victor? You choose.

Who I am is defined by *whose* I am. There is nothing to prove and nothing to protect. I am whose I am. And that is enough.

Several pearls of our identity in Christ can be found in scripture:

> We are loved.[1]
> We are a temple of the Holy Spirit.[2]
> We are adopted into God's family.[3]
> We are God's masterpiece.[4]
> We are whole in Christ.[5]

> *"Again, the kingdom of heaven is like a merchant man, seeking goodly pearls: Who when he had found one pearl of great price, went and sold all that he had, and bought it."*[6]

ENDNOTES

1. Jeremiah 31:3
2. 1 Corinthians 6:19
3. Romans 8:17
4. Ephesians 2:10
5. Colossians 2:10
6. Matthew 13:45-46

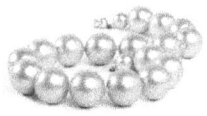

18
pearls of jesus' love

I am humbled by the degree of pain and suffering Jesus endured the day He was crucified. He was betrayed by a close friend, Judas; He endured severe beating; a thorny crown was pressed into His head; He carried His own cross through the town as He was mocked; and finally, He was nailed to that cross and a spear driven through His side, all while innocent of any sin.

That is how much He loves us. Jesus came for two reasons: to die for our sins, and to display the love of Father God. We see this in His lifestyle and ministry and in the tender love and graciousness with which He embraces people who have fallen.

> *"Neither height nor depth, nor anything else in all creation, will be able to separate us from the love of God that is in Christ Jesus our Lord."*[1]

ENDNOTES

1. Romans 8:39

19

pearls of kindness

I lived in Connecticut when the Sandy Hook Elementary School shooting took place. Twenty children and six adults were gunned down by a terrorist. In addition to that tragedy, I experienced one of my own on the very same day. My mother passed away and was in the very same funeral home many of the victims were taken to. One of the small children even had the same birthday as my mother and unfortunately, the same date of death.

It was almost too much to bear. Yet, in the aftermath of the tragedy, an online campaign, led by Ann Curry, grew into the "26 Acts of Kindness,"—an initiative to give back following the Newtown, Connecticut tragedy.

> *"Imagine if all of us committed to one act of kindness; for each precious life lost. An act of kindness; big or small. Are you in?"* [1]
>
> *"People are often unreasonable, irrational, and self-centered.*
>
> *Forgive them anyway.*
>
> *If you are kind, people may accuse you of selfish, ulterior motives.*
>
> *Be kind anyway.*
>
> *If you are successful, you will win some unfaithful friends and some genuine enemies.*
>
> *Succeed anyway.*
>
> *If you are honest and sincere, people may deceive you.*
>
> *Be honest and sincere anyway.*
>
> *What you spend years creating, others could destroy overnight.*
>
> *Create anyway.*
>
> *If you find serenity and happiness, some may be jealous.*

Be happy anyway.

The good you do today, will often be forgotten.

Do good anyway.

Give the best you have, and it will never be enough.

Give your best anyway.

In the final analysis, it is between you and God.

It was never between you and them anyway."[2]

ENDNOTES

1. Sieczkowski, Cavan. "26 Acts of Kindness Campaign Honors Newtown Shooting Victims, Goes Viral." Huffpost, 18 December 2012, www.huffingtonpost.com.

2. Teresa, Mother. "People Are Often Unreasonable and Self-Centered." Healthy Thought.com, http://www.healthythoughts.in. Accessed 11 September 2017.

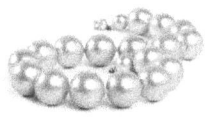

20
pearls of mercy

Some pearls of mercy I noticed along my journey are:

1. My life may not be going the way I planned, but it is going the way God planned.
2. God's light will shine when all else fades.
3. God loves each of us as if there were only one of us.
4. Every day we are offered new mercies from God.

Whatever your situation, God wants to heal you, strengthen you, and lead you to a place where you can enjoy life once again. Recognize that God knows you will require mercy every day, and He is willing and faithful to provide it.

> *"Grace, mercy and peace from God the Father and from Jesus Christ, the Father's Son, will be with us in truth and love."*[1]

ENDNOTES

1. 2 John 1:3

21
pearls of a new name

So, what's in a name? My given name at birth was Margaret Lynn Dearth. As a child, my family called me Peggy. Peggy is a common nickname for Margaret although I never cared for it. I was called "Piggy Peggy" one too many times. When I went to college in 1991, my roommate asked me what nickname I went by. I was thrilled to pick my own very own, Maggie.

Think about it: people called us a name when we were born. Yet, before we were even conceived, God knew us and predestined us.

The promise of being given a new name probably refers to the updated status we have when God begins something new in us. Lots of things are given new names or versions, such as the "new heavens and earth," where the redeemed sing a new song as new creatures who are walking in newness of life.[1]

When we become a child of God, we are called by a new name. Why? Because God wants to establish a new identity for the world to see. God changes Abram's name to Abraham in Genesis 17:5, Jacob's name to Israel in Genesis 32:28, and Simon's name to Peter in John 1:42.

> *"Lord, you are my God. I will exalt you and praise your name, for in perfect faithfulness you have done things, things planned long ago."*[2]

> *"Whoever has ears, let them hear what the Spirit says to the churches. To the one who is victorious, I will give some of the hidden manna. I will also give that person a white stone with a new name written on it, known only to the creator."*[3]

ENDNOTES

1. Isaiah 65:17
2. Isaiah 25:1
3. Revelation 2:17

22

pearls of obedience

Sometimes we may not understand where our journey is taking us. Sometimes the "not knowing" is beautiful. It's beautiful because it expresses the trust within our covenant with God. When we are anchored to Christ and His truth, we can trust the God in us and the God in others.

Sure, we will make mistakes from time to time. That's part of the beauty. Each time we are in His presence, all things become new. The key is to keep our eyes on Christ and cling to the Word of God.

Can it be that easy? Yes, it can. Obedience brings confidence and security because we know we are within the will of God.

How do we know if we are within God's will?[1]

- The door that God opens will never contradict His word.[2]
- The door that God opens will be accompanied by confirmation.[3]
- The door God opens will require you to depend on Him.[4]

> *"To obey is better than sacrifice."*[5]
>
> *"So, Abraham called that place, 'The Lord Will Provide.' And to this day it is said, 'On the Mountain of the Lord it will be provided.'"*[6]

ENDNOTES

1. McMenamin, Cindi. "3 Ways to Know if an 'Open Door' Is from God." Crosswalk.com, http://www.crosswalk.com/faith/women/three-ways-to-know-if-an-open-door-is-from-god.html. Accessed 11 September 2017.

2. Hebrews 10:24

3. Matthew 18:15-16

4. Matthew 6:33

5. 1 Samuel 15:22

6. Genesis 22:14

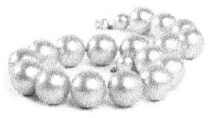

23
pearls of our words

"The power of life and death" is a powerful statement in and of itself. Are we aware of the words that come out of our mouths about others? More importantly, are we aware of what we are speaking over ourselves?

Sometimes we speak so harshly to ourselves out of habit. We say things we would never say to others. Why do we hold ourselves to a different and nearly impossible standard?

As Christians, we know we should do unto others what we wish to be done unto us. It sounds pretty simple and straightforward. However, how can we love others as Christ loves us, if we do not first love ourselves?

Words spoken out loud and words inside our heads are powerful. We must use them to build up and speak life. Jesus declared, "I am a child of God!" and established several characteristics about himself in the book of John through I AM statements. Here are the seven found there:

I AM the bread of life...[1]

I AM the light of the world...[2]

I AM the gate...[3]

I AM the good Shepard...[4]

I AM the resurrection and the life...[5]

I AM the way and the truth and the life...[6]

I AM the true vine...[7]

"I am! Two of the most powerful words we can use! What we put after them can shape our future good or bad."[8]

> *"For we are God's handiwork, created in Christ Jesus to do good works, which God prepared in advance for us to do."*[9]

"The tongue has the power of life and death, and those who love it will eat its fruit."[10]

ENDNOTES

1. John 6:35, 48

2. John 8:12, 9:5

3. John 10:7

4. John 10:14

5. John 11:25

6. John 14:6

7. John 15:1, 5

8. Locken, Lee Ann. Inspiration by Lee Anne Locken.com, http://www.inspirationbyleeannelocken.com. Accessed 4 July 2017.

9. Ephesians 2:10

10. Proverbs 18:21

24
pearls of overcoming distress

In 2010, I had the pleasure of meeting Dr. Marsha Linehan at a conference held at the Institute of Living, in Hartford, CT.

Dr. Linehan is the originator of Dialectical Behavioral Therapy (DBT). I was intrigued to learn that Dr. Linehan had once been a patient at the institute years prior. I felt I could trust her because I believed she understood what I was facing at the time.

I attended a few DBT groups and found them to be very helpful.

I now have four steps during times of distress that help me move past the event and on to what really matters in my life. This is especially important when it relates to my daughter's health, my marriage, and other family relationships.

1. Distress Tolerance: Look for activities that help soothe your senses. Push away disrupting thoughts and emotions.

2. Improve the Moment: Meditate on images, prayers, or scriptures that elevate your level of thinking. Encourage and accept yourself.

3. Practice Mindfulness: Distinguish what is real and what is in your head, and focus on only those things that are within your ability to change.

4. Regulate Your Emotions: Monitor your sleep, nutrition, and exercise, as they all contribute to your overall sense of well-being. Accumulate positive emotions.[1]

> *"I have told you these things, so that in me you may have peace. In this world, you will have trouble. But take heart! I have overcome the world."*[2]

> *"And the peace of God, which transcends all understanding, will guard your hearts and your minds in Christ Jesus."*[3]

ENDNOTES

1. Linehan, Marsha. *DBT Skills Manual, 2nd Edition*. The Guilford Press, 2016.

2. John 16:33

3. Philippians 4:6-7

25
pearls of peace

Some pearls of peace I want to share with you are:

- A heart at peace gives life to the body.
- Faith says no matter what lies ahead, God is already there.
- Don't let the behavior of others destroy your inner peace.
- At the end of each day, give your worries to God and go to sleep.

Happiness can be found even in the darkest of times. There is light, hope, and opportunity waiting. Even on the darkest day, there is light. You just need to search it out.

> "A woman in harmony with her spirit is like a river flowing. She goes where she will without pretense and arrives at her destination prepared to be herself, and only herself."[1]

> "For a child will be born to us, a son will be given to us; And the government will rest on His shoulders; And His name will be called Wonderful Counselor, Mighty God, Eternal Father, Prince of Peace."[2]

> "My Peace I give you; not as the world gives do I give to you. Let not your heart be troubled, neither let it be afraid."[3]

ENDNOTES

1. Maya Angelou. Good Reads.com, https://www.goodreads.com/quotes/106516-a-woman-in-harmony-with-her-spirit-is-like-a. Accessed 11 September 2017.

2. Isaiah 9:6 (NASB)

3. John 14:27 (NASB)

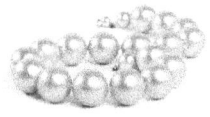

26
pearls of perspective

One thing I really appreciate is perspective. Perspective is simply the way you see things. Sometimes, the view is amazing; other times, it is not, but often just turning around can change your perspective.

God's perspective is big-picture. One godly perspective I now live with every day is that no matter sick or healthy you are, no one is guaranteed tomorrow. All you are promised is this very moment. What are you doing with it?

Since no one is guaranteed a tomorrow, sick or healthy, why not look for the smallest speck of beauty in the smallest things? You can retrain your eyes to see beauty where ever you go. That's called hope. We have today to be inspired and keep moving forward.

> *"Surely goodness and mercy shall follow me all the days of my life, and I shall dwell in the house of the Lord forever."* [1]

ENDNOTES

1. Psalm 23:6 (ESV)

27
pearls of presence

I find great comfort in knowing that God is always with me, for that is one of His promises.

"I will never leave you nor forsake you."[1]

So that means, even in my darkest hour, He is with me, and at my greatest mountain-top moments, He is with me.

Izaak Walton once shared that, "God has two dwellings; one in heaven, and the other in a meek and thankful heart."[2] That is a very powerful image for me. God dwells in you and me, simultaneously. He is omnipresent, fully capable of meeting each of our unique needs.

> *"And why do you worry about clothes? See how the flowers of the field grow. They do not labor or spin. Yet I tell you that not even Solomon in all his splendor was dressed like one of these. If that is how God clothe the grass of the field, which is here today and tomorrow is thrown into the fire, will he not much more clothe you — you of little faith?"*

> *"So do not worry, saying, 'What shall we eat?' or 'What shall we drink?' or 'What shall we wear?' For the pagans run after all these things, and your heavenly Father knows that you need them."*

ENDNOTES

1. Deuteronomy 31:6
2. Walton, Izaak. *The Complete Angler*. CreateSpace, 2009.
3. Matthew 6:27-32

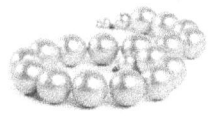

28
pearls of provision

God gave manna to Israel in the wilderness during their exodus from Egypt. A whole nation needed to survive the barren wilderness to reach their promised land, Canaan.

The book of Exodus depicts this journey, and I find it interesting, that this nation witnessed God using Moses. They witnessed the Passover, the plagues, the red sea split, and Pharaoh's army destroyed, but they still questioned whether they were going to eat.

God provided for them. The word manna means, "the miraculous bread of heaven."[1] The people would not have survived without it. God gave them everything they could not provide for themselves, but God expected them to trust and obey Him. That is what He expects from each of us today–to trust and obey.

Jesus is our "bread of life."[2] Jesus, and the things He provides, are to the spirit what physical bread is to the body. He fills the emptiness and satisfies our deep human longings. He instills confidence and hope.

Jesus even refers to eating his flesh and drinking his blood as a metaphor of receiving His word and example into our hearts. Going through the motions won't do it.[3] (John 6:52-58 NIV). We must fully receive Jesus.

> *"Bring the whole tithe into the storehouse, that there may be food in my house. Test me in this, says the Lord Almighty, and see if I will not throw open the flood gates of heaven and pour out so much blessings that you will not have room enough for it."*[4]

> *"The water I give them will become in them a spring of water welling up to Eternal Life."*[5]

> *"But Samuel replied: Does the Lord delight in burnt offerings and sacrifices as much as in*

obeying the Lord? To obey is better than sacrifice, and to heed is better than the fat of rams."[6]

"To him who overcomes, I will give some of the hidden manna to eat."[7]

ENDNOTES

1. "Manna." Bible Study Tools, http://www.biblestudytools.com. Accessed 21 August 2017.
2. John 6:47-51
3. John 6:52-58
4. Malachi 3:10
5. John 4:14
6. 1 Samuel 5:22
7. Revelation 2:17

29

pearls of purpose

Life is a journey with problems to solve and lessons to learn, but most of all, experiences to enjoy. My journey has molded me into the person I am today and taught me to live with purpose. It was exactly what it needed to be. Every good and bad situation has served to bring me to where I am now.

Step one: Survive your childhood.

Hey, we all grew up with some level of dysfunction. Life happens. I believe my parents did the best job they could raising four children. However, I acknowledge that sometimes their best wasn't the best for me. Now, it takes large amounts of courage to press on and overcome.

Step two: Create connections.

If you choose to undertake such a rewarding challenge, first secure your connection with God. Living in denial might make you feel happy momentarily, but that's not joy. Second, secure connections with others. We were never meant to go through life alone. Find your tribe and connect.

Step three: Recognize you are here for a purpose.

This is key for stability and motivation. It stems from your connection to God and funnels into your connection with others.

> *"The moment you began praying, a command was given. And now I am here to tell you what it was, for you are very precious to God. Listen carefully so that you can understand the meaning of your vision."* [1]

ENDNOTES

1. Daniel 9:23 (NLT)

30
pearls of resurrection power

What a joy it is to know who we are in Christ and all that God has placed in us. Christ has sealed us with his precious Holy Spirit. The Bible tells us in Romans 8:11 that the very same spirit that raised Christ from the dead dwells in us. God's power in us can move mountains and bring down kingdoms.

We are all made "more than conquers through Christ that saved us."[1] Absolutely nothing can separate us from the love of God.

In 1 Kings 17, Elijah prays for the rain to be held by the heavens and then prays for the rain to come in 1 Kings 18. Elijah is actively and expectantly looking for change because the Lord had told Elijah that the rain would come.

As we line up our lives through the Holy Spirit and with the word of God, God is faithful to move in our own lives, God can breathe new life into dry bones. As we line up with the word of God, He is faithful to move.

> *"And if The Spirit of him, who raised Jesus from the dead is living in you, he who raised Christ from the dead will also give life to your mortal bodies because of his Spirit who lives in you."*[2]

> *"He will come to us like rain."*[3]

> *"I want to know Christ- yes, to know the power of His resurrection and the participation in His sufferings, becoming like Him in His death."*[4]

ENDNOTES

1. Romans 8:37
2. Romans 8:11
3. Hosea 6:3
4. Philippians 3:10

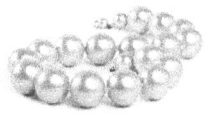

31
pearls of righteousness

What is righteousness? According to *Webster's Dictionary*, it is *"the quality of being morally right or justifiable."* The righteousness of God is the natural expression of His holiness found within His Word.

His Holiness:

"Therefore, since we are receiving a kingdom that cannot be shaken, let us be thankful, and so

worship God acceptably with reverence and awe, for our God is a consuming fire."[2]

His Goodness:

"Taste and see that the Lord is good; blessed is the one who takes refuge in him."[3]

His Justice:

"But you must return to your God, maintain love and justice, and wait for your God always."[4]

Walking in His Holiness:

"I will stand my watch and station myself on the ramparts; I will look to see what he will say to me, and what answer I am to give to this complaint."[5]

"I will go before you and will level the mountains; I will break down gates of bronze and cut through bars of iron. I will give you hidden treasures, so that you may know that I am the Lord, the God of Israel, who summons you by name."[6]

"Blessed are those who hunger and thirst for righteousness, for they will be filled."[7]

ENDNOTES

1. "Righteousness." Webster's New World Dictionary. Ed. Michael Agnes. Wiley Publishing, 2003.

2. Hebrews 12: 28-29 NIV

3. Psalm 34:8

4. Hosea 12:6

5. Habakkuk 2:1

6. Isaiah 45:2-3

7. Matthew 5:5

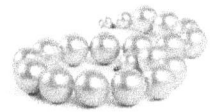

32
pearls of seeking justice

"Justice consists not in being neutral between right and wrong, but in finding out the right and unfolding it, wherever found, against the wrong."[1]

"For You have girded me with strength for battle; You have subdued under me those who rose up against me."[2]

The Holy Bible gives us many examples, in both the Old and New Testament, of great warriors who sought justice. David and Joshua are some of my favorite examples. God can and will use anyone for the advancement of His kingdom! Why not You?

Warriors must put on the full armor of God, found in Ephesians 6:10-18.

Helmet of Salvation
Declare: "Jesus, You are my salvation."

Breastplate of Righteousness
Declare: "Jesus, You are my righteousness."

The Shield of Faith
Declare: "Jesus, You are my faith."

The Belt of Truth
Declare: "Jesus, You are my truth."

Feet Prepared with the Gospel of Peace
Declare: "Jesus, You are my readiness."

The Sword of the Spirit
Declare: "Jesus, You are my Living Word."

Some warriors are called to be watchmen. The word *watcher* is only used in the Holy Bible a few times. To me, being a watchman means to be awake and aware of what is going on.

> *"I saw in the visions of my head as I lay in bed, and behold, a watcher, a holy one, came down from heaven."*[3]

ENDNOTES

1. Roosevelt, Theodore. Good Reads.com, https://www.goodreads.com/quotes/423147-justice-consists-not-in-being-neutral-between-right-and-wrong. Accessed 11 September 2017.

2. Psalm 18:39 (KJV)

3. Daniel 4:13

33
pearls of self-care

As mothers, we want to fix everything, and it can be exhausting. We do for everyone else and leave ourselves as the very last thing on our list.

Self-care is oh-so-important. Taking care of ourselves should be a higher priority than we make it. If we took the time to listen to our bodies, hearts and minds, we would know when they needed rest and rejuvenation. The bottom line is, if we treated ourselves with as much care as we treat our children and good friends, we would likely be a better version of ourselves.

It really is okay to give ourselves a much-needed time out. Sometimes we just need to hit the reset button and move forward.

"Tomorrow is a new day; fresh with no mistakes in them"

"But those who trust in the Lord for help will find their strength renewed, they will rise on wings like eagles; they will run and not get weary; they will walk and not grow weak."

ENDNOTES

1. Montgomery, L. M. *Anne of Green Gables*. Bantam Books, 1976.

2. Isaiah 40:31

34
pearls of service

My daughter, Emma, was diagnosed with multiple autoimmune disorders at the age of ten. I am thankful to God for every moment I share with her and thankful I get to be there to care for her. I saw firsthand that not all parents of chronically ill children can stay with their sick children 24/7. That reality hurt my heart.

After a while, I realized that right before my eyes, my husband was going through that exact same scenario. My husband, Jim, was the reason I could be there for my daughter. He served our family by taking care of our son, Drew, our dog, Tucker, the house, and a full-time job, all the while dealing with the fact that his child was sick, too.

I was able to be with my daughter for every doctor appointment, hospital stay, and ER visit—every scary moment, and every happy moment, including our family's Make a Wish™ CT Adventure to London and Paris, in April of 2016.

My husband's selfless acts of service allowed my daughter and me to have precious time together. I really got to know her, and she got to know me. As a result, a very special and priceless connection formed.

> *"The King will reply, 'Truly I tell you, whatever you did for one of the least of these brothers and sisters of mine, you did for me.'"*[1]

ENDNOTES

1. Matthew 25:40

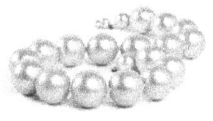

35
pearls of surrender

"One of the happiest moments in life is when you find the courage to let go of what you cannot change." –Unknown

I wonder what would happen if we all gave ourselves permission to just be? To let go? To truly surrender is to lay down every worry, concern, and heartache at the foot of the cross—to let go and just be.

We cannot change the past, nor can we predict what our future holds. We have this moment.

The best yet most difficult choice you can make sometimes is to surrender. That, my friend, brings true peace. This process involves vulnerability. It only hurts when you try to resist what God is doing in your life. It is easier if you just embrace the process and enjoy His peace.

True surrender involves trust. Some people think they have done something so terrible that they try to hide it from God. You can't hide from God. He sees all. There are no secrets with Him. I encourage you all to lean in to Him. Let Him see inside your heart. Let Him see it all, because it is beautiful.

"Owning our story can be hard; but not nearly as difficult as spending our lives running from it. Embracing our vulnerabilities is risky; but not nearly as dangerous as giving up on love and belonging and joy; the experiences that make us the most vulnerable; only when we are brave enough can we explore the infinite power of our light."[1]

> *"Do your best to present yourself to God as one approved worker who does not need to be ashamed. And who correctly handles the word of truth."*[2]
>
> *"Trust in the Lord with all your heart and lean not on your own understanding."*[3]

"Humble yourselves, therefore, under God's mighty hand, that He may lift you up in due time. Cast all your anxiety on him because he cares for you."[4]

ENDNOTES

1. Brown, Brene. *The Gifts of Imperfections: Let go Who You Think You're Supposed to be and Embrace Who You Are*, Hazelden, 2010.

2. 2 Timothy 2:15

3. Proverbs 3:5

4. 1 Peter 5:6-7

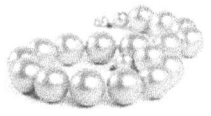

36
pearls of transformation

My past contains a fair share of events that were dark and ripe with chaos. So many things fell apart before my eyes. My life was blown to bits over and over again before the ultimate rebuilding & transformation. And I have to tell you, transformation is brutal.

Transformation does hurt, but it is so worth the peace of Christ. Just like the stages of metamorphosis, transformation gives us the chance at a fresh start as a new creation.

Right now, in this moment, as I breathe this breath, I trust it. I trust these changes I've made despite how hard they've been and as utterly impossible as they once seemed. I wanted extraordinary. And now, I feel the roots of something extraordinary starting to grow.

I feel a tender spring inside. I feel buds of possibility and hope and again. I trust the transformation, and in trusting, I soften. My muscles were relentlessly tense for far too long trying to avoid the process. It actually became easier once I let go and began trusting.

Sometimes, it is embracing who you are and loving yourself with humility that empowers you to transform into all God created you to be. Accepting yourself with all the wrinkles and flaws rather than remaining your own worst enemy creates the fertile soil for new things to grow.

> *"The level of faith and trust that you place in God will determine the size of your victory."*[1]

> *"And we all, who with unveiled faces contemplate the Lord's Glory, are being transformed into his image with ever-increasing glory, which comes from the Lord, who is in the Spirit."*[2]

ENDNOTES

1. Wilson, Yvonne. AskIdeas.com, https://www.askideas.com/63-all-time-best-victory-quotes-sayings/ Accessed 11 September 2017.

2. 2 Corinthians 3:18

37
pearls of trust

Death is sometimes the best proof of life. Conduct is the best proof of character. Mistakes are proof that you are trying. A scar is the proof of a healed wound, and the best proof of love is laying down one's life.

The proof that our relationship is right with God is that we trust.

What is trust? How do we obtain, retain, and regain trust once it has been broken?

It all starts with trusting and believing God knows our end from our beginning, then trusting our part in the process. New levels in life require new trust levels.

Every decision we make in life is made from either love or fear. Never let fear decide your fate. If He brought you to this place, He will be faithful to bring you through it.

> *"But God demonstrates His own love toward us, in that while we were still sinners, Christ died for us."* [1]

ENDNOTES

1. Romans 5:8 (NKJV)

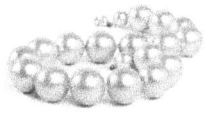

38
pearls of togetherness

Henry Ford once said, "Coming together is a beginning, keeping together is progress, working together is success."[1] "Together" is a wonderful place to be. Blood makes you related, but loyalty makes you family.

Not everyone understands the value or benefits of togetherness. They may even be a little standoffish. You don't have to wait for people to be friendly; rather, you can show them how it's done.

"I appeal to you, brothers and sisters, in the name of our Lord Jesus Christ, that all of you agree with one another in what you say and that there be no divisions among you, but that you be perfectly united in mind and thought."[2]

"How good and pleasant it is when God's people live together in unity."[3]

ENDNOTES

1. Ford, Henry. BrainyQuote.com. https://www.brainyquote.com/quotes/quotes/h/henryford121997.html. Accessed 11 September 2017.

2. 1 Corinthians 1:10

3. Psalm 133:1

39
pearls of unity

The unity we pursue is the unity of truth. We all play a vital role within the body of Christ. When we all truly stand together in unity, we experience a collaborative and collective victory for the advancement of His kingdom. Unity is what will make the church a beacon of light in this dark time.

We are all members of the body of Christ, and when we live like it, we are an unstoppable force. My family experienced this unity in a special way back in 2016. In January of 2016, Chris, a youth pastor at Christ For the Nations Institute (CFNI, which is also my alma mater), began fasting and praying for a child he didn't know. Later that month, someone told him about Emma and her wish to go on a missionary trip to Europe. He looked us up and called me, sharing that Emma was the child he had been fasting and praying for.

He established the "Emma Minute"; every day at a certain time, the entire student body prayed for Emma. The student body even raised funds to fly our entire family to CFNI for a week during their Youth for the Nations camp. They treated us like royalty and with such honor. I felt uncomfortable, unworthy of this kind of care, but they really placed a spiritual covering and blessing on us. I remember one particular girl who accepted salvation at the camp while we were there. It was then that I realized that I had forgotten much of what my identity in Christ was for—the advancement of His kingdom—and I started my journey back to that identity that day.

> *"And over all these virtues put on love, which binds them all together in perfect unity."*[1]
>
> *"Be eager to maintain the unity of the Spirit in the bond of peace."*[2]

ENDNOTES

1. Colossians 3:14 (NKJV)

2. Ephesians 4:3 (RSV)

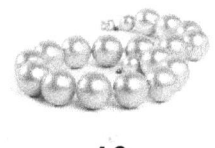

40
pearls of victory

White pebbles were used for several things in the ancient world. In ancient courts, those accused of crimes were acquitted or condemned by vote of a jury, council, or panel. The voting member would cast a white pebble for acquittal or a black pebble for guilty. Members of tribunals condemning Christians cast black stones against them.

At Pergamum, black stones had been cast when judging Antipas, and he was put to death. But Jesus says He will give the one who overcomes a *"white stone."*[1] He declares such a one as vindicated, pure, and guiltless. It does not matter if the world condemns you, if the one who has the keys of death sets you free!

When facing ridicule or worse, remember that the Lord will give you vindication and victory if you overcome by faith.

> *"Therefore, he is able to save completely those who come to God through him, because he always lives to intercede for them."*[2]

> *"What, then, shall we say in response to these things? If God is for us, who can be against us? He who did not spare his own Son, but gave him up for us all- how will he not also, along with him, graciously give us all things?"*[3]

> *"Overcoming by faith means being steadfast, diligent and dedicated. It is to those who overcome that Jesus promises access to the tree of life and that the second death will not hurt them. He also promises hidden manna and a white stone. What wonderful hope these things symbolize!"*[4]

ENDNOTES

1. Revelation 2:17
2. Hebrews 7:25 (NLT)
3. Romans 8:31-32
4. "*The I's of Revelation.*" Warner Home Ministry, 26 December 2016, http://www.warnerministry.com/?s=overcoming+by+faith. Accessed 11 September 2017.

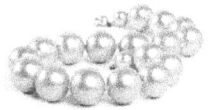

41
pearls of vow-making

A vow contains three key actions:

Sacrifice—adoration, prayer, following the examples of Christ.

Change—your thought patterns and behavior. Believe in yourself!

Offer—your life to God.[1]

On January 1, 2016, I made a vow to my God. I understood

the significance of what a vow truly meant. I was entering, into a covenant with Him, a contract that has many benefits. Because I understood the commitment, and the value of my actions within the covenant, I could remain stable during the stormy seas of life. I could hold fast to each promise from God, written in His Word.

I sacrificed by fasting and praying. I changed bad habits and offered Him my praise. I waited patiently and silently, with a spirit of thanksgiving, while I received from the Holy Spirit.

> *"But now, this is what the LORD says - He who created you, Jacob, He who formed you, Israel: 'Do not fear, for I have redeemed you; I have summoned you by name; You are Mine.'"*[2]
>
> *"Where you go, I will go, where you stay, I will stay."*[3]

ENDNOTES

1. Backford, Ashley. "The Vow Challenge/ Fully Devoted Worship," http://www.ashleybeckford.wordpress.com. Accessed March 6, 2017.

2. Isaiah 43:1

3. Ruth 1:16

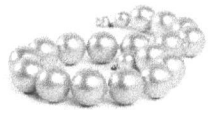

42
pearls of worth

I have realized something so significant this past year: I am enough! Even with my prickles and flaws that make me who I am, I am enough. I have found there is power in being vulnerable, and that it takes much less energy to embrace who you are than hide from it.

I am more aware that I am a deeply sensitive person and that for the most part, this is a positive trait. I have found my tribe through church and deep relationships and am learning that it can be a wonderful thing to let a good friend see into my heart.

On this journey, I have learned that you cannot grasp anything new if your hands are full of yesterday's garbage. It is okay to let go in pursuit of becoming everything God has created you to be. Let go of the past, and soon enough it will let go of you.

When in doubt, focus on God's promises. This is key for a viable relationship with Christ. Have faith in your journey and what it is producing in your life. Everything had to happen to get you to where you are now. Embrace the future that God has planned for you and enjoy life.

You Are God's Masterpiece, Fearfully and Wonderfully Made.

> *"I praise you because I am fearfully and wonderfully made; Your works are wonderful, I know that full well."* [1]

ENDNOTES

1. Psalm 139:14

about the author

Maggie Jamieson is a wife, mother, and loyal friend with a strong and passionate spiritual ministry. Her ministry education began at Christ for the Nations Institute in Dallas, Texas in 1991. She graduated with a degree in theology and became a director of children's ministry.

Her vocational work has been centered around the spiritual growth and education of children. Through ministry, she was able to experience her own personal healing from traumatic events from her past.

As Maggie continues her healing journey, she has a strong commitment to help others overcome life-changing traumatic events. Her writings are a true testament of God's power.

Maggie lives with her husband Jim and their two children, Emma and Drew, in Branford, Connecticut.

www.MaggieJamieson.org

WORKS CITED

Maya Angelou. *Good Reads.com,* https://www.goodreads.com/quotes/106516-a-woman-in-harmony-with-her-spirit-is-like-a. Accessed 11 September 2017.

Backford, Ashley. "The Vow Challenge/ Fully Devoted Worship," http://www.ashleybeckford.wordpress.com. Accessed March 6, 2017.

The Bible. *English Standard Version. Biblehub.com.* Biblehub, 2016. http://biblehub.com. Accessed 16 August 2017.

The Bible. *King James Version. Biblehub.com.* Biblehub, 2016. http://biblehub.com. Accessed 16 August 2017.

The Bible. *The Living Bible. Biblehub.com.* Biblehub, 2016. http://biblehub.com. Accessed 16 August 2017.

The Bible. *New American Standard. Biblehub.com.* Biblehub, 2016. http://biblehub.com. Accessed 16 August 2017.

The Bible. *New International Version. Biblehub.com.* Biblehub, 2016. http://biblehub.com. Accessed 16 August 2017.

The Bible. *New King James Version. Biblehub.com.* Biblehub, 2016. http://biblehub.com. Accessed 16 August 2017.

The Bible. *New Living Translation. Biblehub.com.* Biblehub,

2016. http://biblehub.com. Accessed 16 August 2017.

The Bible. *Revised Standard Version. Biblehub.com.* Biblehub, 2016. http://biblehub.com. Accessed 16 August 2017.

Brown, Brene. "14 Inspirational Quotes from Brene Brown." *Happily Imperfect.com*, edited by Sharon Martin. Accessed 11 September 2017.

Brown, Brene. *The Gifts of Imperfections: Let go Who You Think You're Supposed to be and Embrace Who You Are*, Hazelden, 2010.

Brown, Brene. *Good Reads.com,* https://www.goodreads.com/quotes/330217-i-now-see-how-owning-our-story-and-loving-ourselves. Accessed 11 September 2017.

"Covenant." *Dictionary.com,* http://www.dictionary.com/browse/covenant. Accessed 7 September 2017.

Ford, Henry. *BrainyQuote.com,* https://www.brainyquote.com/quotes/quotes/h/henryford121997.html. Accessed 11 September 2017.

Linehan, Marsha. *DBT Skills Manual*, 2nd Edition. The Guilford Press, 2016.

Locken, Lee Ann. *Inspiration by Lee Anne Locken.com,* http://www.inspirationbyleeannelocken.com. Accessed 4 July 2017.

"Manna." *Bible Study Tools,* http://www.biblestudytools.com. Accessed 21 August 2017.

McMenamin, Cindi. "3 Ways to Know if an "Open Door" Is from God." *Crosswalk.com,* http://www.crosswalk.com/faith/women/three-ways-to-know-if-an-open-door-is-from-god.html. Accessed 11 September 2017.

Montgomery, L. M. *Anne of Green Gables.* Bantam Books, 1976.

"The I's of Revelation." *Warner Home Ministry,* 26 December 2016, http://www.warnerministry.com/?s=overcoming+by+faith. Accessed 11 September 2017.

Roosevelt, Theodore. *Good Reads.com,* https://www.goodreads.com/quotes/423147-justice-consists-not-in-being-neutral-between-right-and-wrong. Accessed 11 September 2017.

"Righteousness." *Webster's New World Dictionary.* Ed. Michael Agnes. Wiley Publishing, 2003.

Robbins, Anthony. *Positively Positive.com.* http://www.positivelypositive.com/?s=Anthony+Robbins&post_type=quotes. Accessed 24 June 2017.

Russell, Pastor Paul. Sermon: *Men and God.*

www.facebook.com/ChristFamilyTV. Accessed June 18, 2017.

Sieczkowski, Cavan. "26 Acts of Kindness Campaign Honors Newtown Shooting Victims, Goes Viral." *Huffpost*, 18 December 2012, www.huffingtonpost.com.

Ten Boom, Corrie. *Brainy Quotes.com,* https://www.brainyquote.com/quotes/quotes/c/corrietenb393675.html. Accessed 11 September 2017.

Teresa, Mother. "People Are Often Unreasonable and Self-Centered." *Healthy Thought.com*, http://www.healthythoughts.in. Accessed 11 September 2017.

Von Balthasar, Hans Urs. *Good Reads.com,* https://www.goodreads.com/author/quotes/30796.Hans_Urs_von_Balthasar. Accessed 11 September 2017.

Walton, Izaak. *The Complete Angler*. CreateSpace, 2009.

Wilson, Yvonne. *AskIdeas.com,* https://www.askideas.com/63-all-time-best-victory-quotes-sayings/. Accessed 11 September 2017.

All scriptures are taking from the New International Version of the Bible unless otherwise noted.

www.ingramcontent.com/pod-product-compliance
Lightning Source LLC
Chambersburg PA
CBHW071705040426
42446CB00011B/1917